LIFE'S LITTLE BOOK OF
WISDOM FOR
Friends

BARBOUR
PUBLISHING

The best mirror is an old friend.

GEORGE HERBERT

FOR WHERE YOUR TREASURE IS,
THERE WILL YOUR HEART BE ALSO.

MATTHEW 6:21 KJV

Hold a true friend with both your hands.

NIGERIAN PROVERB

Don't walk in front of me, I may not follow;
Don't walk behind me, I may not lead;
Walk beside me, and just be my friend.

Albert Camus

FRIENDS TOUCH OUR LIVES
IN WAYS NO ONE ELSE CAN. . . .
THEY LEAVE LASTING IMPRINTS ON OUR HEARTS.

K. WILLIAMS

TO LOVE IS TO PLACE OUR HAPPINESS
IN THE HAPPINESS OF ANOTHER.

GOTTFRIED WILHELM VON LEIBNIZ

Who, being loved, is poor?

OSCAR WILDE

*The greatest sweetener
of human life is friendship.*

JOSEPH ADDISON

OUR MOUTHS WERE FILLED WITH LAUGHTER,
OUR TONGUES WITH SONGS OF JOY.

PSALM 126:2 NIV

Laughter is the sun that drives winter from the face.

VICTOR HUGO

GOD GIVES US LOVE;
SOMETHING TO LOVE HE LENDS US.

ALFRED, LORD TENNYSON

The love we give away
is the only love we keep.

ELBERT HUBBARD

IT'S SUBLIME TO FEEL AND SAY OF ANOTHER...

I RELY ON HIM AS ON MYSELF.

RALPH WALDO EMERSON

IF YOU CAN EAT TODAY,
ENJOY THE SUNLIGHT TODAY,
MIX GOOD CHEER WITH FRIENDS TODAY,
ENJOY IT AND BLESS GOD FOR IT.

HENRY WARD BEECHER

HE WHO SOWS COURTESY REAPS FRIENDSHIP,
AND HE WHO PLANTS KINDNESS GATHERS LOVE.

ST. BASIL

WE LIVE BY ADMIRATION, HOPE, AND LOVE.

WILLIAM WORDSWORTH

A friend loveth at all times.

PROVERBS 17:17 KJV

HAPPINESS IS SOMETHING TO DO,
SOMETHING TO LOVE,
SOMETHING TO HOPE FOR.

CHINESE PROVERB

A heart in tune with God is a heart that beats for others.

BONNIE JENSEN

Joy is the net of love
by which you can catch souls.

MOTHER TERESA

"LOVE THY NEIGHBOR" IS A PRECEPT
WHICH COULD TRANSFORM THE WORLD
IF IT WERE UNIVERSALLY PRACTICED.

MARY MCLEOD BETHUNE

I FIND EACH DAY TOO SHORT FOR ALL THE
THOUGHTS I WANT TO THINK, ALL THE WALKS I
WANT TO TAKE, ALL THE BOOKS I WANT TO READ,
ALL THE FRIENDS I WANT TO SEE.

JOHN BURROUGHS

OINTMENT AND PERFUME REJOICE THE HEART:
SO DOTH THE SWEETNESS OF
A MAN'S FRIEND BY HEARTY COUNSEL.

PROVERBS 27:9 KJV

INTO ALL LIVES, IN MANY SIMPLE, FAMILIAR,
HOMELY WAYS, GOD INFUSES THIS ELEMENT
OF JOY FROM THE SURPRISES OF LIFE,
WHICH UNEXPECTEDLY BRIGHTEN OUR DAYS,
AND FILL OUR EYES WITH LIGHT.

HENRY WADSWORTH LONGFELLOW

There are times when encouragement means a lot. And a word is enough to convey it.

GRACE STRICKER DAWSON

ONE WHO KNOWS HOW TO SHOW AND
TO ACCEPT KINDNESS WILL BE A FRIEND
BETTER THAN ANY POSSESSION.

SOPHOCLES

*Laughter need not be cut out of anything,
since it improves everything.*

JAMES THURBER

Blessed are those who
give without remembering
and receive without forgetting.

UNKNOWN

It is a comely fashion to be glad—
joy is the grace we say to God.

JEAN INGELOW

*So encourage each other
to build each other up,
just as you are already doing.*

1 THESSALONIANS 5:11 TLB

THE LIVES THAT HAVE BEEN THE
GREATEST BLESSING TO YOU ARE THE LIVES
OF THOSE PEOPLE WHO THEMSELVES WERE
UNAWARE OF HAVING BEEN A BLESSING.

OSWALD CHAMBERS

*That action is best
which procures the greatest
happiness for the greatest numbers.*

FRANCIS HUTCHESON

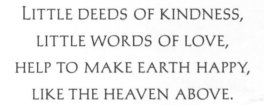

LITTLE DEEDS OF KINDNESS,
LITTLE WORDS OF LOVE,
HELP TO MAKE EARTH HAPPY,
LIKE THE HEAVEN ABOVE.

J. FLETCHER CARNEY

When grace is joined with wrinkles, it is adorable. There is an unspeakable dawn in happy old age.

VICTOR HUGO

THE MORE WE LOVE, THE BETTER WE ARE;
AND THE GREATER OUR FRIENDSHIPS ARE,
THE DEARER WE ARE TO GOD.

JEREMY TAYLOR

IF ONE FALLS DOWN, HIS FRIEND CAN HELP HIM UP.
BUT PITY THE MAN WHO FALLS AND
HAS NO ONE TO HELP HIM UP!

ECCLESIASTES 4:10 NIV

FRIENDS ARE AS COMPANIONS ON A JOURNEY
WHO OUGHT TO AID EACH OTHER TO
PERSEVERE IN THE ROAD TO A HAPPIER LIFE.

PYTHAGORAS

Good company upon the road
is the shortest cut.

ANONYMOUS

MY FRIEND IS NOT PERFECT—NOR AM I—
AND SO WE SUIT EACH OTHER ADMIRABLY.

ALEXANDER POPE

*The greatest pleasure I know
is to do a good action.*

CHARLES LAMB

I HAD THREE CHAIRS IN MY HOUSE:
ONE FOR SOLITUDE, TWO FOR FRIENDSHIP. . . .

HENRY DAVID THOREAU

A real friend helps us think our best thoughts, do our noblest deeds, be our finest selves.

UNKNOWN

48

FRIENDSHIP IS UNNECESSARY, LIKE PHILOSOPHY,
LIKE ART. . . . IT HAS NO SURVIVAL VALUE;
RATHER IS ONE OF THOSE THINGS THAT
GIVES VALUE TO SURVIVAL.

C. S. LEWIS

I ALWAYS THANK MY GOD AS
I REMEMBER YOU IN MY PRAYERS.

PHILEMON 1:4 NIV

Cheerfulness is the offshoot of goodness.

CHRISTIAN NESTELL BOVEE

IT IS NOT PART OF GOD'S PLAN THAT
EACH ONE OF US HAS BEAUTY OR FAME.
BUT I BELIEVE HE DID INTEND FOR ALL
OF US TO KNOW THE KINDNESS
AND COMPASSION OF A FRIEND.

ANITA WIEGAND

Cultivate solitude and quiet and a
few sincere friends, rather than mob
merriment, noise, and thousands of
nodding acquaintances.

William Powell

*The greatest healing therapy
is friendship and love.*

HUBERT HUMPHREY

A GOOD LAUGH MAKES US BETTER FRIENDS
WITH OURSELVES AND EVERYBODY AROUND US.

ORISON MARDEN

IF WE WOULD BUILD ON A SURE FOUNDATION
IN FRIENDSHIP, WE MUST LOVE FRIENDS FOR
THEIR SAKE RATHER THAN FOR OUR OWN.

CHARLOTTE BRONTË

The best things in life are never rationed.
Friendship, loyalty, love
do not require coupons.

GEORGE T. HEWITT

Depth of friendship does not depend on length of acquaintance.

Sir Rabindranath Tagore

THOSE WHO BRING SUNSHINE TO THE LIVES
OF OTHERS CANNOT KEEP IT FROM THEMSELVES.

JAMES M. BARRIE

IT IS THROUGH KINDNESS AND COMPASSION
THAT HEARTS CONNECT AND FRIENDSHIP BEGINS.

BONNIE JENSEN

KEEP ON LOVING EACH OTHER. . . .
DO NOT FORGET TO ENTERTAIN STRANGERS,
FOR BY SO DOING SOME PEOPLE HAVE
ENTERTAINED ANGELS WITHOUT KNOWING IT.

HEBREWS 13:1-2 NIV

THE BEST THINGS ARE NEAREST:
BREATH IN YOUR NOSTRILS, LIGHT IN YOUR EYES,
FLOWERS AT YOUR FEET, DUTIES AT YOUR HAND,
THE PATH OF GOD JUST BEFORE YOU.

ROBERT LOUIS STEVENSON

Optimism is the faith that leads to achievement. Nothing can be done without hope and confidence.

HELEN KELLER

INDEED, WE DO NOT REALLY LIVE UNLESS WE HAVE
FRIENDS SURROUNDING US LIKE A FIRM WALL
AGAINST THE WINDS OF THE WORLD.

CHARLES HANSON TOWNE

In prosperity our friends know us;
in adversity we know our friends.

JOHN CHURTON COLLINS

ENJOY THE LITTLE THINGS,
FOR ONE DAY YOU MAY LOOK BACK
AND DISCOVER THEY WERE THE BIG THINGS.

UNKNOWN

Familiar acts are beautiful through love.

PERCY BYSSHE SHELLEY

All God's angels come to us disguised.

JAMES RUSSELL LOWELL

True prayer is not to be found in the words of the mouth but in the thoughts of the heart.

When you rise in the morning,
form a resolution to make the day
a happy one to a fellow friend.

SYDNEY SMITH

LOVE IS AN IMAGE OF GOD, AND NOT A LIFELESS IMAGE, BUT THE LIVING ESSENCE OF THE DIVINE NATURE WHICH BEAMS FULL OF ALL GOODNESS.

MARTIN LUTHER

My coat and I live comfortably together. It has assumed all my wrinkles, does not hurt me anywhere, has molded itself on my deformities, and is complacent to all my movements, and I only feel its presence because it keeps me warm. Old coats and old friends are the same thing.

Victor Hugo

Walking with a friend in the dark is better than walking alone in the light.

HELEN KELLER

SOME PEOPLE COME INTO OUR LIVES,
LEAVE FOOTPRINTS ON OUR HEARTS,
AND WE ARE NEVER THE SAME.

UNKNOWN

May the Lord continually bless you
with heaven's blessings as well
as with human joys.

PSALM 128:5 TLB

BE THE LIVING EXPRESSION OF GOD'S KINDNESS:
KINDNESS IN YOUR FACE,
KINDNESS IN YOUR EYES,
KINDNESS IN YOUR SMILE.

MOTHER TERESA

We cannot really love anybody
with whom we never laugh.

AGNES REPPLIER

A friend is one who knows you and loves you just the same.

ELBERT HUBBARD

I HAVE FRIENDS IN OVERALLS WHOSE FRIENDSHIP
I WOULD NOT SWAP FOR THE FAVOR
OF THE KINGS OF THE WORLD.

THOMAS A. EDISON

IF INSTEAD OF A GEM, OR EVEN A FLOWER,
WE SHOULD CAST THE GIFT OF A LOVING
THOUGHT INTO THE HEART OF A FRIEND,
THAT WOULD BE GIVING AS THE ANGELS GIVE.

GEORGE MACDONALD

For the happy heart,
life is a continual feast.

PROVERBS 15:15 NLT

We cannot tell the precise moment when friendship is formed. As in filling a vessel drop by drop, there is at last a drop which makes it run over. So in a series of kindness there is, at last, one which makes the heart run over.

James Boswell

In everyone's life, at some time,
our inner fire goes out. It is then burst
into flame by an encounter with another
human being. We should all be thankful
for those people who rekindle the inner spirit.

Albert Schweitzer

LET US BE GRATEFUL TO PEOPLE WHO MAKE
US HAPPY; THEY ARE THE CHARMING GARDENERS
WHO MAKE OUR SOULS BLOSSOM.

MARCEL PROUST

Hand grasps hand, eye lights eye in good friendship, and great hearts expand, and grow. . . .

ROBERT BROWNING

Long years apart can make
no breach a second cannot fill.

EMILY DICKINSON

IT IS IN THE SHELTER OF
EACH OTHER THAT PEOPLE LIVE.

IRISH PROVERB

TRUST SHOULD BE IN THE LIVING GOD
WHO ALWAYS RICHLY GIVES US
ALL WE NEED FOR OUR ENJOYMENT.

1 TIMOTHY 6:17 TLB

BUT FRIENDSHIP IS PRECIOUS, NOT ONLY IN THE
SHADE, BUT IN THE SUNSHINE OF LIFE; AND THANKS
TO A BENEVOLENT ARRANGEMENT OF THINGS,
THE GREATER PART OF LIFE IS SUNSHINE.

THOMAS JEFFERSON

Friendship takes fear from the heart.

GEORGE ELIOT

FRIENDS PUT THE ENTIRE WORLD
TO RIGHT OVER A CUP OF TEA.

CHARLOTTE GRAY

A friend is the hope of the heart.

RALPH WALDO EMERSON

IN WHAT SEEMS ORDINARY AND EVERYDAY
THERE IS ALWAYS MORE THAN
AT FIRST MEETS THE EYE.

CHARLES CUMMINGS

It is great to have friends when one is young,
but indeed it is still more so when you are
getting old. When we are young, friends are,
like everything else, a matter of course.
In the old days, we know what
it means to have them.

Edvard Grieg

THE MOST BEAUTIFUL DISCOVERY THAT TRUE
FRIENDS CAN MAKE IS THAT THEY CAN GROW
SEPARATELY WITHOUT GROWING APART.

ELIZABETH FOLEY

A sweet friendship refreshes the soul.

PROVERBS 27:9 MSG

HAPPINESS IS A HABIT; CULTIVATE IT.

ELBERT HUBBARD

One enemy is too many;
a hundred friends too few.

ANONYMOUS

I HAVE LEARNED THAT TO HAVE A GOOD FRIEND
IS THE PUREST OF ALL GOD'S GIFTS, FOR IT IS
A LOVE THAT HAS NO EXCHANGE OF PAYMENT.

FRANCES FARMER

How unspeakably the lengthening of memories in common endears our old friends!

GEORGE ELIOT

THE WORLD IS SO EMPTY IF ONE THINKS ONLY
OF THE MOUNTAINS, RIVERS, AND CITIES;
BUT TO KNOW SOMEONE WHO THINKS AND FEELS
WITH US, AND WHO, THOUGH DISTANT IS CLOSE
TO US IN SPIRIT, THIS MAKES THE EARTH
FOR US AN INHABITED GARDEN.

JOHANN WOLFGANG VON GOETHE

To love and be loved is to feel the sun from both sides.

DAVID VISCOTT

FRIENDSHIP THAT FLOWS FROM THE HEART
CANNOT BE FROZEN BY ADVERSITY,
AS THE WATER THAT FLOWS FROM THE
SPRING CANNOT CONGEAL IN WINTER.

JAMES FENIMORE COOPER

TREAT YOUR FRIENDS AS YOU DO YOUR PICTURES,
AND PLACE THEM IN THEIR BEST LIGHT.

SIR WINSTON CHURCHILL

GOD HAS GIVEN EACH OF YOU SOME SPECIAL
ABILITIES; BE SURE TO USE THEM TO HELP
EACH OTHER, PASSING ON TO OTHERS
GOD'S MANY KINDS OF BLESSINGS.

1 PETER 4:10 TLB

Love is best of all.
There is not, nor ever shall there be,
true friendship without it.

UNKNOWN

THINK WHERE MAN'S GLORY MOST BEGINS
AND ENDS, AND SAY MY GLORY WAS
I HAD SUCH FRIENDS.

WILLIAM BUTLER YEATS

My friends are little lamps to me,
Their radiance warms and cheers my ways,
and all the pathway dark and lone
is brightened by their rays.

Elizabeth Whittemore

TRUE FRIENDSHIP IS A PLANT OF SLOW GROWTH,
AND MUST UNDERGO AND WITHSTAND
THE SHOCKS OF ADVERSITY BEFORE IT
IS ENTITLED TO THE APPELLATION.

GEORGE WASHINGTON

Unshared joy is an unlighted candle.

SPANISH PROVERB

FRIENDSHIP IS BORN AT THAT MOMENT
WHEN ONE PERSON SAYS TO ANOTHER:
"WHAT! YOU, TOO?
I THOUGHT I WAS THE ONLY ONE."

C. S. LEWIS

NO DISTANCE OF PLACE OR LAPSE OF TIME
CAN LESSEN THE FRIENDSHIP OF THOSE WHO
ARE THOROUGHLY PERSUADED OF
EACH OTHER'S WORTH.

ROBERT SOUTHEY

BE SLOW TO FALL INTO FRIENDSHIP;
BUT WHEN THOU ART IN,
CONTINUE FIRM AND CONSTANT.

SOCRATES

THE GLORY OF FRIENDSHIP IS. . .
THE SPIRITUAL INSPIRATION THAT COMES TO
ONE WHEN HE DISCOVERS THAT SOMEONE ELSE
BELIEVES IN HIM AND IS WILLING TO
TRUST HIM WITH HIS FRIENDSHIP.

RALPH WALDO EMERSON

By friendship you mean the greatest love, the greatest usefulness, the most open communication, the noblest sufferings, the severest truth, the heartiest counsel, and the greatest union of minds which brave men and women are capable.

Jeremy Taylor

The heart that loves
is always young.

GREEK PROVERB

A REAL FRIEND WARMS YOU BY
HER PRESENCE, TRUSTS YOU WITH
HER SECRETS, AND REMEMBERS
YOU IN HER PRAYERS.

UNKNOWN

DO ALL THE GOOD YOU CAN,
BY ALL THE MEANS YOU CAN,
IN ALL THE WAYS YOU CAN,
AT ALL THE TIMES YOU CAN,
TO ALL THE PEOPLE YOU CAN,
AS LONG AS EVER YOU CAN.

JOHN WESLEY

THERE ARE TWO THINGS ONE SHOULD
KNOW ABOUT THE DIRECTION OF LIFE.
FIRST IS: WHERE AM I GOING?
SECOND IS: WHO WILL GO WITH ME?

ELIE WIESEL

*True friendship isn't measured by time,
but by the times shared.*

KELLY EILEEN HAKE

TO HAVE A GOOD FRIEND IS ONE OF THE HIGHEST
DELIGHTS OF LIFE; TO BE A GOOD FRIEND IS
ONE OF THE NOBLEST UNDERTAKINGS.

UNKNOWN

*A word spoken in due season,
how good is it!*

PROVERBS 15:23 KJV

TO BE GLAD OF LIFE, BECAUSE IT GIVES YOU
THE CHANCE TO LOVE AND TO WORK AND TO
PLAY AND TO LOOK UP AT THE STARS. . .TO THINK
SELDOM OF YOUR ENEMIES, OFTEN OF YOUR FRIENDS,
AND EVERY DAY OF CHRIST. . .THESE ARE LITTLE
GUIDEPOSTS ON THE FOOTPATH OF PEACE.

HENRY VAN DYKE

You cannot always have happiness,
but you can always give happiness.

UNKNOWN

THE KINGDOM OF HEAVEN IS OF THE CHILDLIKE,
OF THOSE WHO ARE EASY TO PLEASE,
WHO LOVE AND GIVE PLEASURE.

ROBERT LOUIS STEVENSON

THE BEST PORTIONS OF A GOOD LIFE ARE THE
LITTLE, NAMELESS, UNREMEMBERED ACTS
OF KINDNESS AND LOVE WE DO FOR OTHERS.

WILLIAM WORDSWORTH

I DO NOT WISH TO TREAT FRIENDSHIPS DAINTILY,
BUT WITH THE ROUGHEST COURAGE. WHEN THEY
ARE REAL, THEY ARE NOT GLASS THREADS OR
FROSTWORK, BUT THE SOLIDEST THING WE KNOW.

RALPH WALDO EMERSON

A PERSON SHOULD HEAR A LITTLE MUSIC,
READ A LITTLE POETRY, AND SEE A FINE PICTURE
EVERY DAY OF THEIR LIFE, IN ORDER THAT
WORLDLY CARES MAY NOT OBLITERATE THE
SENSE OF THE BEAUTIFUL WHICH GOD HAS
IMPLANTED IN THE HUMAN SOUL.

JOHANN WOLFGANG VON GOETHE

Flowers are lovely; love is flower—like.
Friendship is a sheltering tree.

SAMUEL TAYLOR COLERIDGE

VERILY, GREAT GRACE MAY GO WITH
A LITTLE GIFT; AND PRECIOUS ARE ALL
THINGS THAT COME FROM FRIENDS.

THEOCRITUS

When friends meet, hearts warm.

ENGLISH PROVERB

INSTEAD OF BEING UNHAPPY, JUST LET YOUR
LOVE GROW AS GOD WANTS IT TO GROW.
SEEK GOODNESS IN OTHERS. LOVE MORE
PERSONS MORE. . .MORE UNSELFISHLY,
WITHOUT THOUGHT OF RETURN. THE RETURN,
NEVER FEAR, WILL TAKE CARE OF ITSELF.

HENRY DRUMMOND

*I find true friendship to be. . .
the true. . .restorative cordial.*

THOMAS JEFFERSON

TRUE FRIENDS DON'T SPEND TIME GAZING INTO EACH OTHER'S EYES. THEY MAY SHOW GREAT TENDERNESS TOWARD EACH OTHER, BUT THEY FACE IN THE SAME DIRECTION— TOWARD COMMON PROJECTS, INTERESTS, GOALS—ABOVE ALL, TOWARD A COMMON LORD.

C. S. LEWIS

A happy heart makes the face cheerful.

PROVERBS 15:13 NIV

WHAT A THING FRIENDSHIP IS,
WORLD WITHOUT END!
HOW IT GIVES THE HEART AND
SOUL A STIR-UP!

ROBERT BROWNING

Do you know that conversation is one of the greatest pleasures in life?

W. SOMERSET MAUGHAM

THE ONLY REWARD OF VIRTUE IS VIRTUE;
THE ONLY WAY TO HAVE A FRIEND IS TO BE ONE.

RALPH WALDO EMERSON

A faithful friend is an image of God.

LIFE IS A CHRONICLE OF FRIENDSHIP.
FRIENDS CREATE THE WORLD ANEW EACH DAY.
WITHOUT THEIR LOVING CARE, COURAGE WOULD
NOT SUFFICE TO KEEP HEARTS STRONG FOR LIFE.

HELEN KELLER

GOD DOES NOTICE US, AND HE WATCHES OVER US.
BUT IT IS USUALLY THROUGH ANOTHER
PERSON THAT HE MEETS OUR NEEDS.

SPENCER W. KIMBALL

149

FILL {YOUR FRIENDS'} LIVES WITH SWEETNESS.
SPEAK APPROVING, CHEERING WORDS WHILE
THEIR EARS CAN HEAR THEM. AND WHILE THEIR
HEARTS CAN BE THRILLED AND MADE HAPPIER.
THE KIND OF THINGS YOU MEAN TO SAY
WHEN THEY ARE GONE, SAY BEFORE THEY GO.

GEORGE W. CHILDS

A FRIEND IS ONE TO WHOM ONE MAY POUR OUT
ALL THE CONTENTS OF ONE'S HEART, CHAFF AND
GRAIN TOGETHER, KNOWING THAT THE GENTLEST
OF HANDS WILL TAKE AND SIFT IT, KEEP WHAT
IS WORTH KEEPING AND WITH A BREATH
OF KINDNESS BLOW THE REST AWAY.

ARABIAN PROVERB

IT IS ONLY WITH THE HEART
THAT ONE CAN SEE RIGHTLY;
WHAT IS ESSENTIAL IS INVISIBLE TO THE EYE.

ANTOINE DE SAINT-EXUPERY

HE WRAPS YOU IN GOODNESS—BEAUTY ETERNAL.
HE RENEWS YOUR YOUTH—YOU'RE ALWAYS
YOUNG IN HIS PRESENCE.

PSALM 103:5 MSG

A friend is someone who knows the song in your heart and can sing it back to you when you have forgotten the words.

UNKNOWN

THE MOST I CAN DO FOR MY
FRIEND IS SIMPLY TO BE HIS FRIEND.
I HAVE NO WEALTH TO BESTOW ON HIM.
IF HE KNOWS THAT I AM HAPPY IN LOVING HIM,
HE WILL WANT NO OTHER REWARD.
IS NOT FRIENDSHIP DIVINE IN THIS?

HENRY DAVID THOREAU

As old wood is best to burn,
old horse to ride, old books to read. . .so are
old friends always most trusty to use.

Leonard Wright

HUMAN LOVE AND THE DELIGHTS OF FRIENDSHIP,
OUT OF WHICH ARE BUILT THE MEMORIES THAT
ENDURE, ARE ALSO TO BE TREASURED UP AS
HINTS OF WHAT SHALL BE HEREAFTER.

BEDE JARRETT

BLESSED ARE THEY WHO HAVE THE GIFT OF MAKING
FRIENDS, FOR IT IS ONE OF GOD'S BEST GIFTS.
IT INVOLVES MANY THINGS, BUT ABOVE ALL
THE POWER OF GOING OUT OF ONE'S SELF
AND APPRECIATING WHAT IS NOBLE
AND LOVING IN ANOTHER.

THOMAS HUGHES

TWO PERSONS CANNOT LONG BE FRIENDS IF THEY
CANNOT FORGIVE EACH OTHER'S LITTLE FAILINGS.

JEAN DE LA BRUYERE

"LET US JOURNEY ON OUR WAY,
AND I WILL GO ALONGSIDE YOU."

GENESIS 33:12 NRSV

Friendship. . . .a union of spirits,
a marriage of hearts.

WILLIAM PENN

A TRUE TEST OF FRIENDSHIP—
TO SIT OR WALK WITH A FRIEND
FOR AN HOUR IN PERFECT SILENCE
WITHOUT WEARYING OF ONE
ANOTHER'S COMPANY.

DINAH MULOCK CRAIK

NOTHING MAKES THE EARTH SEEM SO
SPACIOUS AS TO HAVE FRIENDS AT A DISTANCE:
THEY MAKE THE LATITUDES AND LONGITUDES.

HENRY DAVID THOREAU

A friend may well be reckoned a masterpiece of nature.

RALPH WALDO EMERSON

I DON'T MEDDLE WITH WHAT MY FRIENDS BELIEVE
OR REJECT, ANY MORE THAN I ASK WHETHER
THEY ARE RICH OR POOR; I LOVE THEM.

JAMES RUSSELL LOWELL

LOVE IS A CHOICE—NOT SIMPLY
OR NECESSARILY A RATIONAL CHOICE,
BUT RATHER A WILLINGNESS TO BE PRESENT
TO OTHERS WITHOUT PRETENSE OR GUILE.

CARTER HEYWARD

God has given us these times of joy.

PSALM 81:4 TLB

MANY A MAN HAS BEEN SAVED FROM A LIFE
OF FRIVOLITY AND EMPTINESS TO A CAREER
OF NOBLE SERVICE BY FINDING AT A CRITICAL
HOUR THE RIGHT KIND OF FRIEND.

G. D. PRENTICE

THE KEY IS TO KEEP COMPANY WITH PEOPLE
WHO UPLIFT YOU, WHOSE PRESENCE
CALLS FORTH YOUR BEST.

ELIZABETH WILLET

Life is fortified by many friendships.

SYDNEY SMITH

FRIENDSHIP IS SOMETHING THAT RAISES US
ALMOST ABOVE HUMANITY. . . . IT IS THE SORT
OF LOVE ONE CAN IMAGINE BETWEEN ANGELS.

C. S. LEWIS

DEAR FRIENDS, NO MATTER HOW WE FIND
THEM, ARE AS ESSENTIAL TO OUR LIVES
AS BREATHING IN AND BREATHING OUT.

LOIS WYSE

Few delights can equal the mere presence of one whom we can trust utterly.

George MacDonald

You have made known to me the path of life;
you will fill me with joy in your presence,
with eternal pleasures at your right hand.

Psalm 16:11 NIV

ADVICE IS LIKE SNOW. THE SOFTER IT FALLS,
THE LONGER IT DWELLS AND THE DEEPER
IT SINKS INTO THE MIND AND HEART.

SAMUEL TAYLOR COLERIDGE

What is a friend?
A single soul in two bodies.

ARISTOTLE

YOUR BEST FRIEND IS THE PERSON WHO BRINGS
OUT OF YOU THE BEST THAT IS WITHIN YOU.

HENRY FORD

A TRUE FRIEND IS THE GIFT OF GOD AND. . .
HE ONLY WHO MADE HEARTS CAN UNITE THEM.

ROBERT SOUTH

Insomuch as any one pushes you nearer to God, he or she is your friend.

FRENCH PROVERB

MY FRIEND SHALL FOREVER BE MY FRIEND,
AND REFLECT A RAY OF GOD TO ME.

HENRY DAVID THOREAU

Friendship, gift of heaven,
pleasure of great souls!

VOLTAIRE

GOOD UNDERSTANDING WINS FAVOR.

PROVERBS 13:15 NIV

*To me, fair friend,
you never can be old.*

WILLIAM SHAKESPEARE

ONLY FRIENDS WILL TELL YOU THE TRUTHS
YOU NEED TO HEAR TO MAKE THE LAST
PART OF YOUR LIFE BEARABLE.

FRANCINE DUPLESSIX GRAY

When you're with a friend,
your heart has come home.

EMILY FARBER

True friendships are lasting
because true love is eternal.
A friendship in which heart
speaks to heart is a gift from God.

HENRI NOUWEN

THE BEST THAT WE FIND IN OUR TRAVELS
IS AN HONEST FRIEND. HE IS A FORTUNATE
VOYAGER WHO FINDS MANY.

ROBERT LOUIS STEVENSON

DEAR FRIEND,
I PRAY THAT YOU MAY ENJOY GOOD HEALTH
AND THAT ALL MAY GO WELL WITH YOU.

3 JOHN 1:2 NIV

THE LANGUAGE OF FRIENDSHIP IS
NOT WORDS, BUT MEANINGS.
IT IS AN INTELLIGENCE ABOVE LANGUAGE.

HENRY DAVID THOREAU

Life is short. Be swift to love;
make haste to be kind.

HENRI F. AMIEL

LAUGHTER IS NOT AT ALL A BAD BEGINNING
FOR A FRIENDSHIP, AND IT IS FAR
THE BEST ENDING FOR ONE.

OSCAR WILDE